PIANO ACCOMPANIMENT

Elementary Scales
AND
Bowings

for STRINGS

by H A R V E Y S . W H I S T L E R and H E R M A N A . H U M M E L

C O N T E N T S

RUBANK®

HAL•LEONARD®
CORPORATION
7777 W. BLUEMOUND RD. P.O. BOX 13819 MILWAUKEE, WI 53213

Key of C Major

Détaché Scale

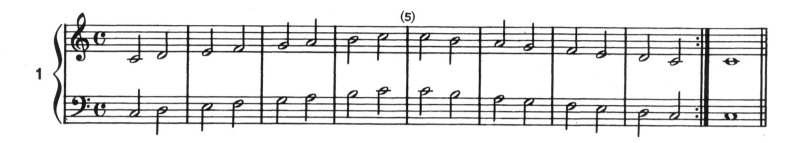

Slurred Scales

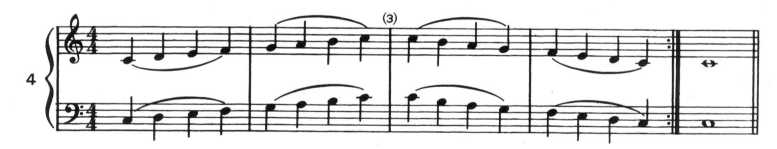

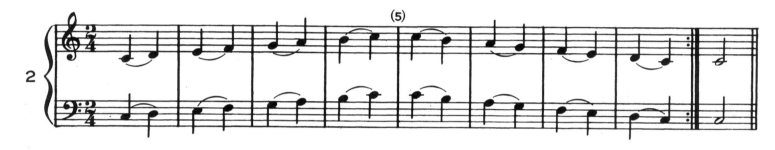

Detached Bowings

1416-23

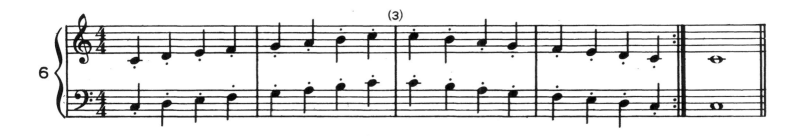

Bow Division

Détaché Scale in Quarter Notes

Broken Chords

Tone Study

Eighth Notes

Quarter and Eighth Notes

1416-23

Key of G Major

Détaché Scale

Slurred Scales

Detached Bowings

22

Bow Division

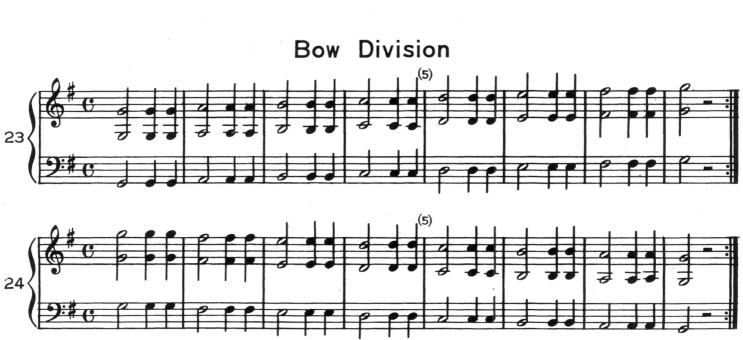

23

24

Détaché Scale in Quarter Notes

25

Broken Chords

26

27

1416-23

Tone Study

Eighth Notes

Quarter and Eighth Notes

Key of D Major

Détaché Scale

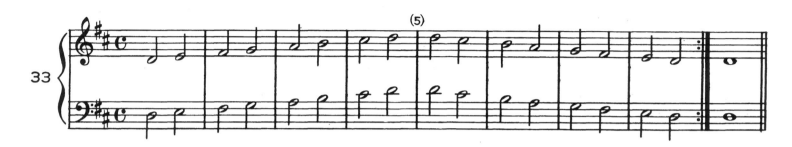

Slurred Scales

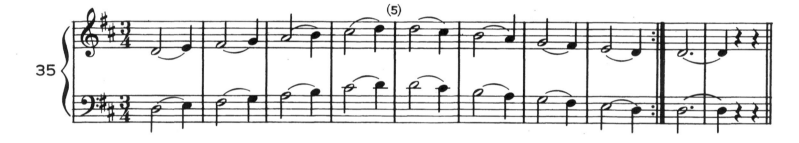

Detached Bowings

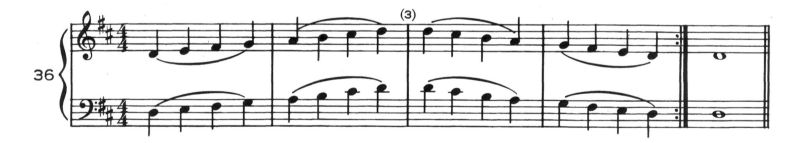

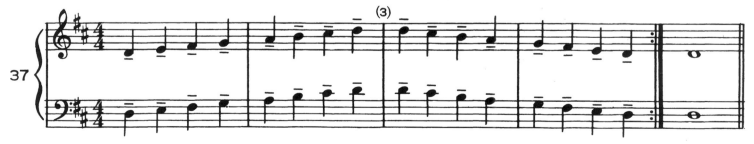

1416-23

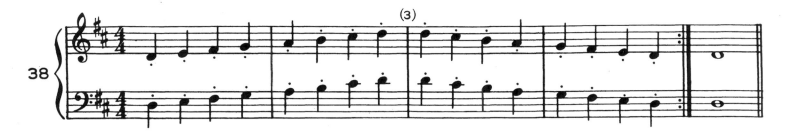

Bow Division

Détaché Scale in Quarter Notes

Broken Chords

Tone Study

Eighth Notes

Quarter and Eighth Notes

1416-23

Key of A Major

Détaché Scale

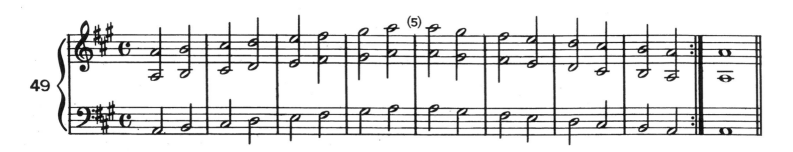

Slurred Scales

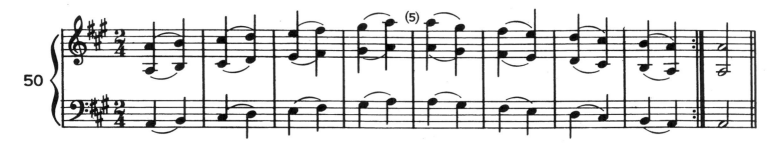

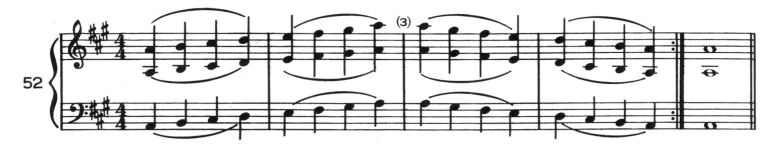

Detached Bowings

Bow Division

Détaché Scale in Quarter Notes

Broken Chords

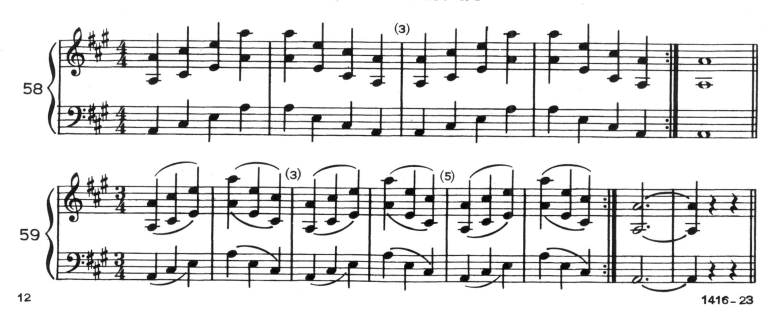

12

Tone Study

Eighth Notes

Quarter and Eighth Notes

Key of F Major

Détaché Scale

Slurred Scales

Detached Bowings

1416-23

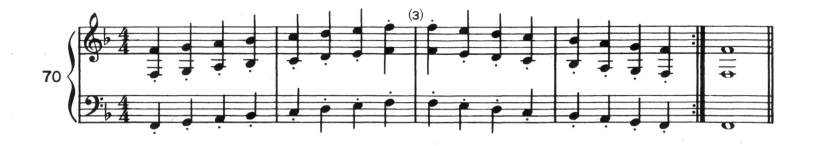

Bow Division

Détaché Scale in Quarter Notes

Broken Chords

Tone Study

Eighth Notes

Quarter and Eighth Notes

Key of B♭ Major

Détaché Scale

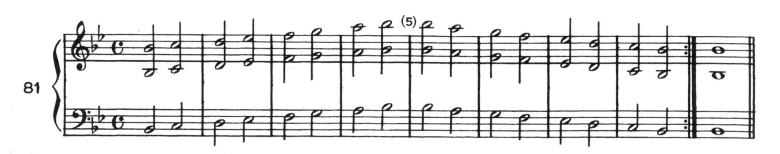

81

Slurred Scales

82

83

Detached Bowings

84

85

Bow Division

Détaché Scale in Quarter Notes

Broken Chords

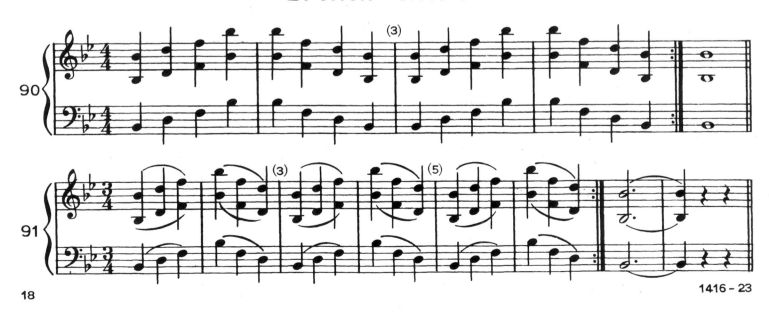

1416-23

Tone Study

Eighth Notes

Quarter and Eighth Notes

Key of E♭ Major

Détaché Scale

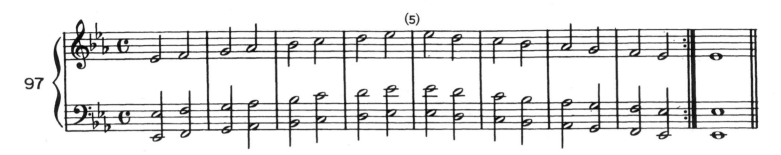

Slurred Scales

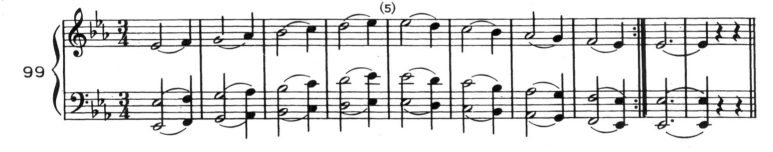

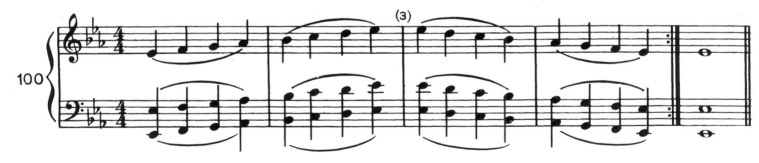

Detached Bowings

1416-23

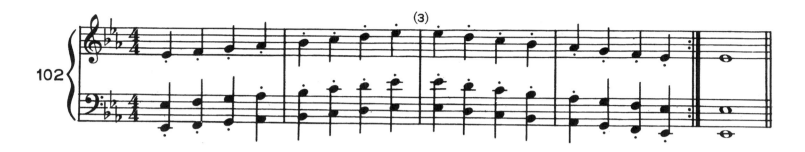

Bow Division

Détaché Scale in Quarter Notes

Broken Chords

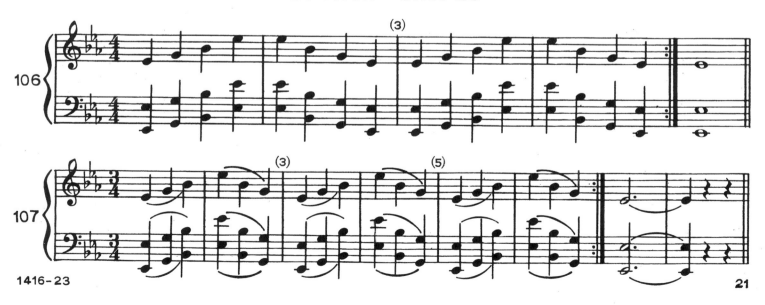

Tone Study

Eighth Notes

Quarter and Eighth Notes

Chromatic Scales

Extended Chromatic Scale

24